Treasure
For Our
Sand Castle

Written by
Chuck Robinson and Debbie Robinson

Illustrated by April Wengren

Colored by _____
This book was illustrated to be enjoyed as is,
or you may add additional colors.

Old Squan Village Publishing
Manasquan, New Jersey

Published by: Old Squan Village Publishing
18 Willow Way, Suite 23
Manasquan, NJ 08736-2835 USA
732-223-9325

Text and Illustrations Copyright © 1997 by Chuck Robinson and Debbie Robinson
First Printing, 1997
Printed in the United States of America

Publisher's Cataloging in Publication Data
Robinson, Chuck.
Treasure for our sand castle / by Chuck Robinson and Debbie Robinson; illustrated by April Wengren.
p.   cm.
Summary: Two children build a big and beautiful sand castle. One child is the narrator as they both explore the beach looking for treasure. They find many interesting seashells and other sea life, soon realizing they found the castle's treasure all along their walk.
1. Seashells —Juvenile literature. 2. Seashore —Juvenile literature. 3. Beachcombing —Juvenile literature.
I. Title. II. Robinson, Debbie.
Library of Congress Catalogue Card Number: 96-72259
594.147'7 —dc21
ISBN 0-9647267-7-7

Our Heartfelt Thanks To:

Dr. Judith Icklan for her enthusiastic interest and help with our literary projects.

April Wengren for her professional insight, advice, and illustrations.

The illustrations for this book were done in pen and ink and tinted with acrylics.
Cover design and illustration concepts were the joint effort of the authors and illustrator.

I love the beach.
It is my favorite place to play and explore.
I like to build sand castles with my friend.
The wet sand near the water is the best sand to use.

It is fun to dig in the sand.
Sometimes we even find mole crabs.
They live in the wet sand where they dig and look for food.

The sand castle we built today is big and beautiful.
Let's decorate it with treasure.
Walk along the beach with me to see what we can find.
The King and Queen will be so pleased when they move in.

Look, a moon shell.
I like it because it is colorful.
It has light blue, white, and yellow swirls.
This shell is empty.
Let's take it back to our sand castle.

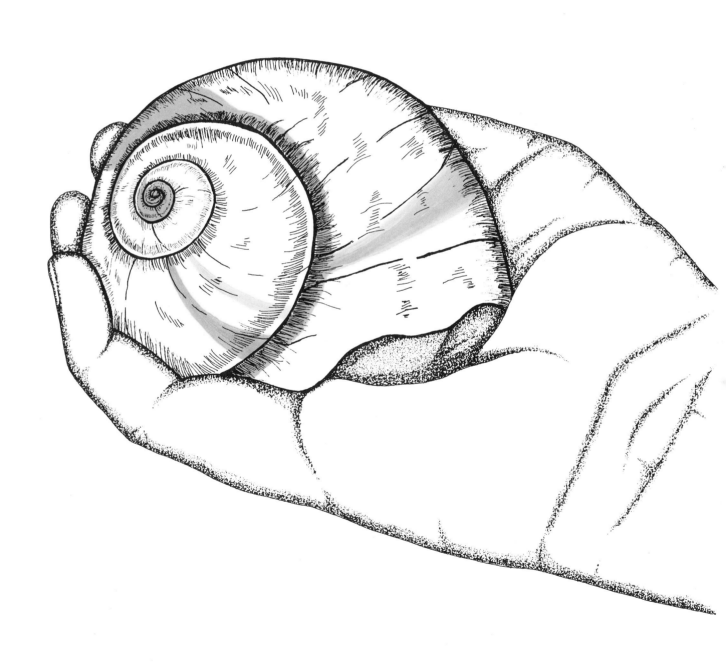

Shells provide a safe home for animals called mollusks.
Mollusks are soft and do not have a spine.
They live in their shell and make their shell bigger as they grow.
Mollusks are always attached to their shell.
Some mollusks move along the ocean floor.
Others dig straight down into the sand.

Snails are mollusks that can go part of the way out of their shell.
They go back into their shell when they get frightened.
Snails have a trap door to close off their opening.
This helps protect the animal.

There are many big surf clam shells on this beach.
We like to paint the shells and give them to our friends.
This shell is only half of the mollusk's shell.
The other half looks the same.
When the animal is alive, the two shells are attached.
The clam closes both halves to protect it from the sea gulls.
Sea gulls love to eat clams.

Look at that sea gull.
It is flying with a sea star in its mouth.
Sea gulls also love to eat sea stars.
Sea stars are marine animals.
They have skeletons and are covered with skin.

Here is a sea star.
It has been dried by the sun.
Although it is not alive, it is beautiful.
There are many interesting things on the beach.
Now if only we could find some treasure.

Look! There is a balloon floating on the water.
Come on, let's get it.
Sea turtles will think it is a jelly fish and they will eat it.
If they eat it, it could kill them.
I hope everyone helps to keep our ocean clean.

Is that a sea horse over there on the sand?
Sea horses live in the ocean near the shore.
They swim by moving their small back fin.
When they want to turn, they move small fins near their ears.
The fin under their belly helps them to stay up straight.
Sometimes strong winds and currents wash sea horses onto the beach.
Sea horses can live only in the water.
I found one on the beach and brought it to school for show and tell.
Everyone at school was excited to learn about this animal.

Come with me to the jetty.
The jetty is a group of big rocks protecting the mouth of the river.
Ocean currents swirl around the jetty.
Shells, stones, and sea life get caught in the rocks.
Maybe we will find some treasure here.

Do you see all the crabs?
Lots of crabs live in the water around the jetty.
Here they can hide from danger and safely search for food.
Crabs are not mollusks, but they have shells too.
I have seen the Atlantic Rock Crab, Blue Crab, and the Spider
Crab.
The Spider Crab has very long legs.
The Blue Crab has blue legs.
The shell of the Atlantic Rock Crab blends in with the rocks.
Sometimes I find crab shells on the beach.

There are many shells here today.
Waves wash over the sand and uncover shells buried below the surface.
Here is a mussel shell. It is black and blue on the outside and a beautiful pearly white on the inside.
Let's keep this one for our collection.

Wow, these scallop shells are very beautiful.
See all the different colors.
Scallop shells are pink, white, and grey.
Some are dark red and white.
Others are dark brown and light brown.
It is fun to decorate things with scallop shells.

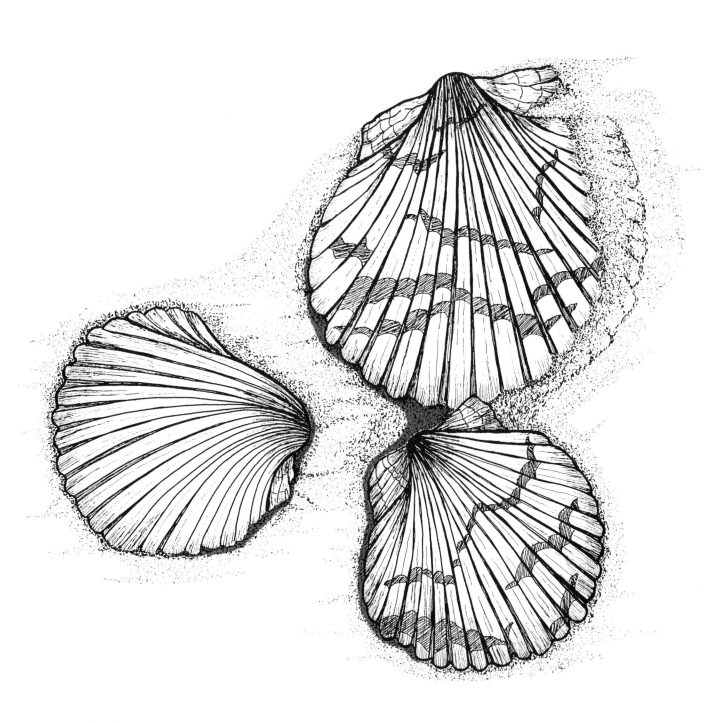

I think it is time to go back to our sand castle.
I hope we find some treasure.
Look over there! A slipper shell.
It looks like a little slipper.
Let's take a few back to our sand castle.

Hurry, over here.
Look at all the stones.
Stones get tumbled around by the waves and break.
The pieces grind together.
They get smaller and smaller.
This makes sand.
Most sand has little pieces of shells in it too.

A big whelk shell just washed onto the beach.
It is one of my favorite shells.
Sometimes the inside of its opening is orange.
The outside of the shell is white or grey and brown.
Its points look like a king's crown.
The whelk shell is big.
It grows up to nine inches long.
Put the opening to your ear and you can hear the ocean.
It is a beautiful shell.   A real treasure.
Did I say "a real treasure?"

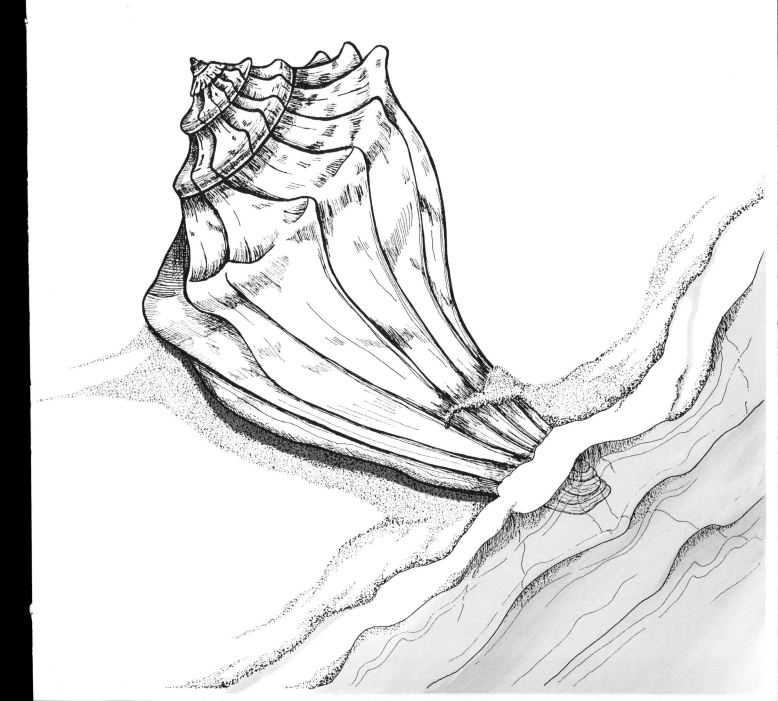

Look at all our treasures!
We were finding the castle's treasure all along our walk, but we didn't even know it.
I wonder if the King and Queen have moved in yet.
Hurry! Let's get back to our sand castle.

Glossary

BLUE CRAB

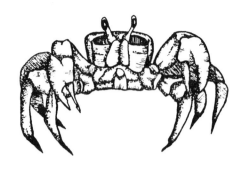

GHOST CRAB

MOLE CRAB

MOON SHELL

MUSSEL SHELL

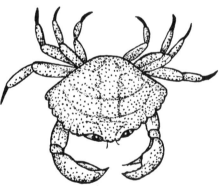

ROCK CRAB

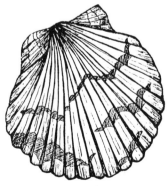

SCALLOP SHELL

SEA HORSE

SEA STAR

SLIPPER SHELL

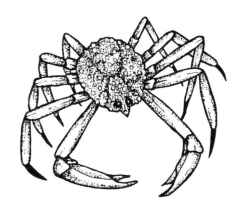

SPIDER CRAB

SURF CLAM

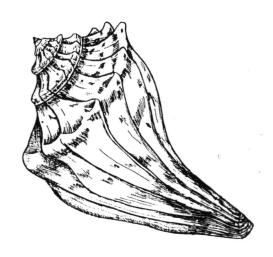

WHELK SHELL

Authors

Chuck and Debbie Robinson have been interested in seashells and the seashore since childhood. They both grew up on the New Jersey shore and together they have been combing beaches since 1984.

Chuck Robinson is an avid writer and photographer. Two of his popular slide presentations are entitled "Atlantic Coast Seashells" and "Treasure For Our Sand Castle." Debbie Robinson has a Bachelor of Arts Degree in Psychology and a Master of Science Degree in Education. She is a director at Ocean County College, Toms River, New Jersey.

The Robinsons are active with many nature groups. They enjoy sharing their knowledge of seashells and the seashore environment through slide presentations and beach walks. Chuck and Debbie Robinson are also the authors of *The ART of SHELLING: A complete guide to finding shells and other beach collectibles at shelling locations from Florida to Maine.*

Illustrator

April Wengren graduated magna cum laude from Kutztown University, Kutztown Pennsylvania, with a Bachelor of Fine Arts degree in Painting. She also studied weaving and fiber design. Her work has been honored with numerous awards to include "Best Collaboration," Dana Gallery, Franklin and Marshall College, Lancaster, Pennsylvania and the "John Guise Memorial Award," Fiber Arts Show, Packwood House, Lewisburg, Pennsylvania. April has had her work exhibited at Bucknell University for the Mid-Atlantic Fiber Conference and at Bloomsburg University as part of a "Two Person Show" in the President's lounge. She was also the illustrator for the Robinson's guidebook *The ART of SHELLING.*

Always alert to her artistic instincts, April is currently working in pen and ink illustrations and experimenting with other media in illustrating. She especially enjoys illustrating children's books.

Text Consultant

Dr. Judith Icklan made her debut in non-academic free lance editing with the Robinsons' first book *The ART of SHELLING.* She holds Masters Degrees in English and in Reading Specialization and a Ph.D. in Rhetoric and Linguistics. This opportunity to work with a children's book satisfied her particular interest in readability. Currently the Associate Vice-President of Academic Affairs at Ocean County College in Toms River, New Jersey, Dr. Icklan has strayed from her earlier creative writing pursuits into the world of reports, memos, and schedules. She looks forward to the day the Robinsons tire of writing books on shelling and the seashore so they can embark on a truly fascinating topic--CATS!